D1064963

COOL CASTLES AND PALACES

PALACE
OF VERSAILLES

by Clara Bennington

Ideas for Parents and Teachers

Pogo Books let children practice reading informational text while introducing them to nonfiction features such as headings, labels, sidebars, maps, and diagrams, as well as a table of contents, glossary, and index.

Carefully leveled text with a strong photo match offers early fluent readers the support they need to succeed.

Before Reading

- "Walk" through the book and point out the various nonfiction features. Ask the student what purpose each feature serves.
- Look at the glossary together. Read and discuss the words.

Read the Book

- Have the child read the book independently.
- Invite him or her to list questions that arise from reading.

After Reading

- Discuss the child's questions. Talk about how he or she might find answers to those questions.
- Prompt the child to think more. Ask: Did you know about the Palace of Versailles before you read this book? What more would you like to learn about it?

Pogo Books are published by Jump!
5357 Penn Avenue South
Minneapolis, MN 55419
www.jumplibrary.com

Library of Congress Cataloging-in-Publication Data

Names: Bennington, Clara, author.
Title: Palace of Versailles / by Clara Bennington.
Description: Pogo books edition.
Minneapolis, MN: Jump!, Inc., [2020]
Series: Cool castles and palaces
Includes index. | Audience: Ages 7-10.
Identifiers: LCCN 2018055993 (print)
LCCN 2019000643 (ebook)
ISBN 9781641288729 (ebook)
ISBN 9781641288712 (hardcover : alk. paper)
Subjects: LCSH: Château de Versailles (Versailles, France)
Juvenile works. Classification: LCC DC801.V55 (ebook)
LCC DC801.V55 B45 2020 (print) | DDC 944/.3663—dc23
LC record available at https://lccn.loc.gov/2018055993

Editor: Jenna Trnka
Designer: Molly Ballanger

Photo Credits: John_Silver/Shutterstock, cover; Asier Villafranca/Shutterstock, 1; photomaster/Shutterstock, 3; 4X5 Collection/SuperStock, 4; Takashi Images/Shutterstock, 5, 10-11; Avillfoto/Shutterstock, 6-7; walter_g/Shutterstock, 8; Hemis/Alamy, 9; Isogood_patrick/Shutterstock, 12-13; Kiev.Victor/Shutterstock, 14; andre quinou/Shutterstock, 15; Pack-Shot/Shutterstock, 16-17, 18-19; Bokstaz/Shutterstock, 20-21; Ligak/Shutterstock, 23.

Printed in the United States of America at Corporate Graphics in North Mankato, Minnesota.

TABLE OF CONTENTS

CHAPTER 1

FRANCE'S LARGEST PALACE

Louis XIV became king of France in 1643. He wanted an extravagant palace.

King Louis XIV

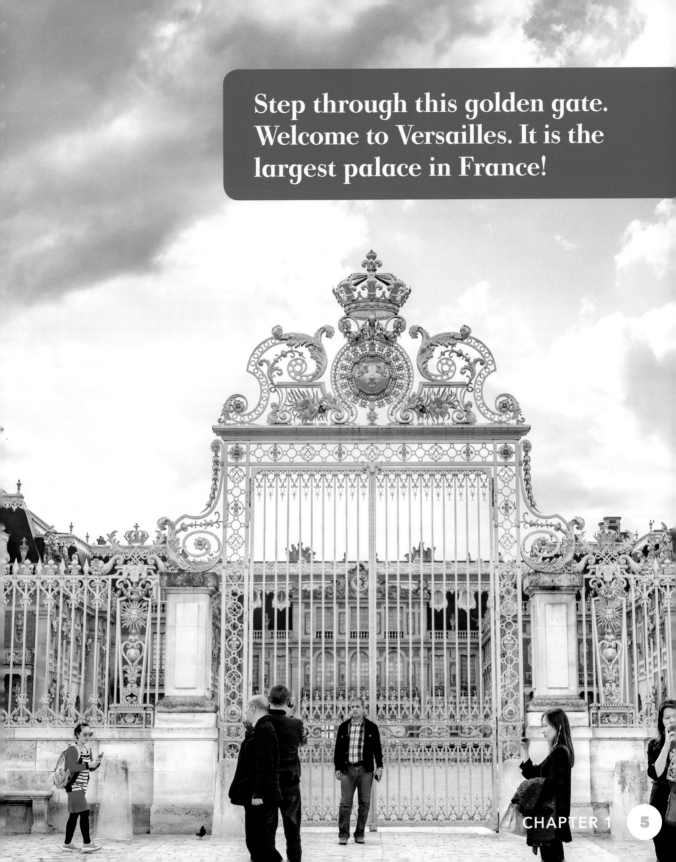

Step through this golden gate. Welcome to Versailles. It is the largest palace in France!

Building started in 1661. More than 36,000 people helped build it. It took more than 50 years to finish. In 1682, King Louis XIV moved in. He made the palace the center of the government. On some days, more than 10,000 people were here!

WHAT DO YOU THINK?

King Louis XIV was known as the Sun King. Why? He chose Apollo, the god of the sun, as his **emblem**. He believed his **reign** cast light over the entire world. Do you think the sun is a good emblem for a king? Why or why not?

CHAPTER 2

INSIDE THE PALACE

Inside the palace are 2,300 rooms! Paintings hang on the walls. **Artisans** were hired to decorate rooms. Beautiful furniture fills them.

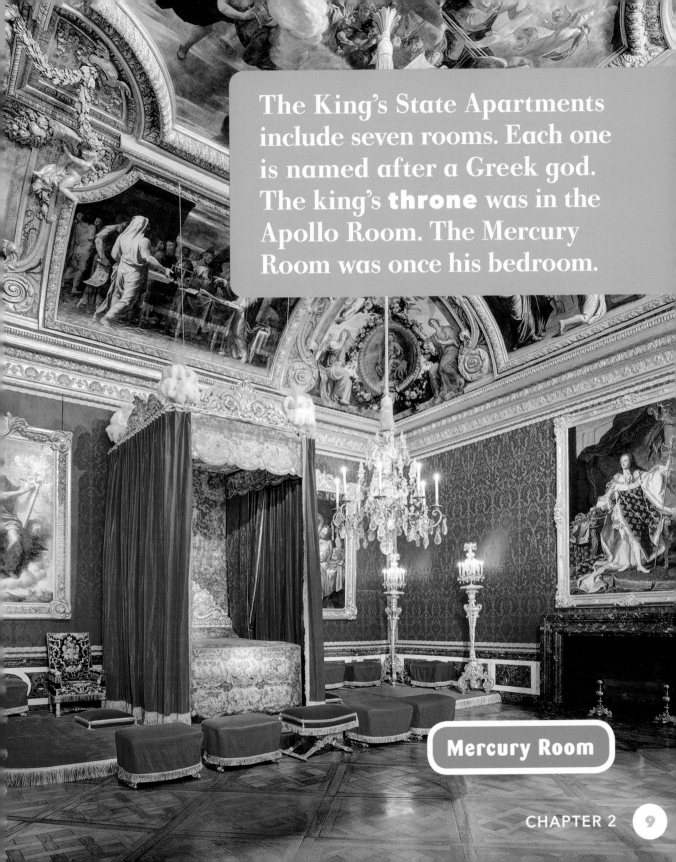

The King's State Apartments include seven rooms. Each one is named after a Greek god. The king's **throne** was in the Apollo Room. The Mercury Room was once his bedroom.

Mercury Room

The Hall of Mirrors is full of light. The 17 arches are covered in 357 mirrors. Large windows face them. Glass chandeliers hang down. Above them, the ceiling is painted.

DID YOU KNOW?

The Hall of Mirrors is famous. Why? The **Treaty** of Versailles was signed here. Why was this treaty important? It ended World War I (1914–1918).

Hall of Mirrors

Royal Opera House

The palace is very **lavish**. Almost all of the kingdom's money was spent on it. Some say it may have cost more than $506 billion dollars in today's money to build!

The **Royal** Opera House was especially lavish. Shows, weddings, and balls took place here.

WHAT DO YOU THINK?

Many people in France were poor. They did not live like the kings and queens. Do you think it was fair for kings and queens to have so much?

CHAPTER 3

A SPRAWLING ESTATE

The king wanted gardens as beautiful as the palace. There were once 1,400 fountains and pools here. Today, there are 55.

Fountain of Apollo

The gardens took more than 40 years to create! See **topiaries**. Statues and palm trees are here, too.

topiary

Grand Trianon

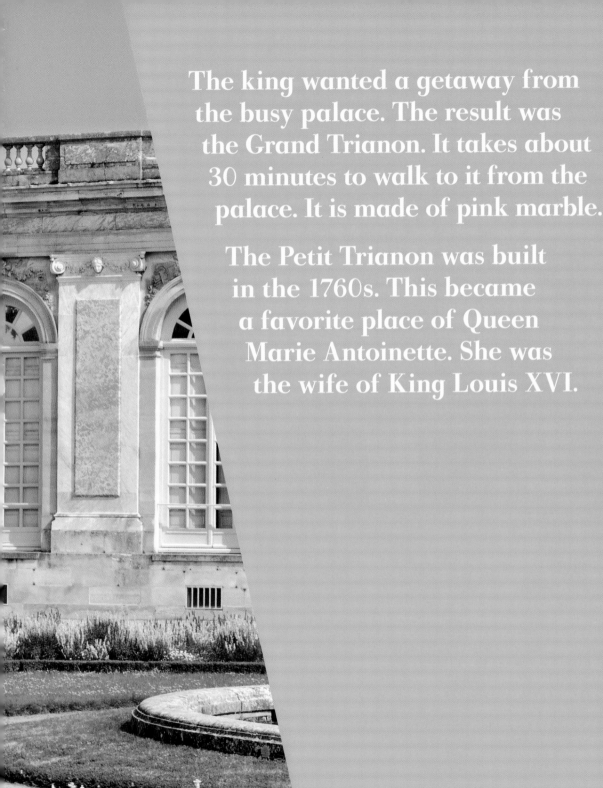

The king wanted a getaway from the busy palace. The result was the Grand Trianon. It takes about 30 minutes to walk to it from the palace. It is made of pink marble.

The Petit Trianon was built in the 1760s. This became a favorite place of Queen Marie Antoinette. She was the wife of King Louis XVI.

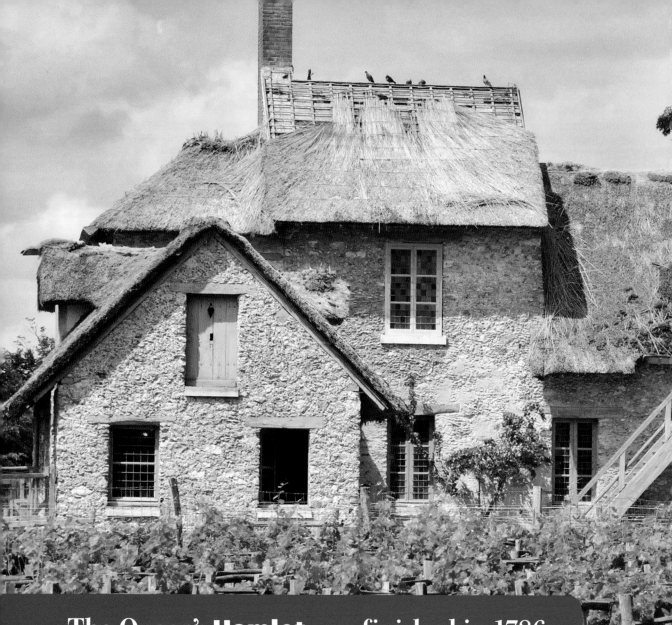

The Queen's **Hamlet** was finished in 1786. The cottages were richly furnished. But this was also a working farm with animals. Some say the queen used it to teach her children about farming.

TAKE A LOOK!

Versailles is a large **estate**. What does it include? Take a look!

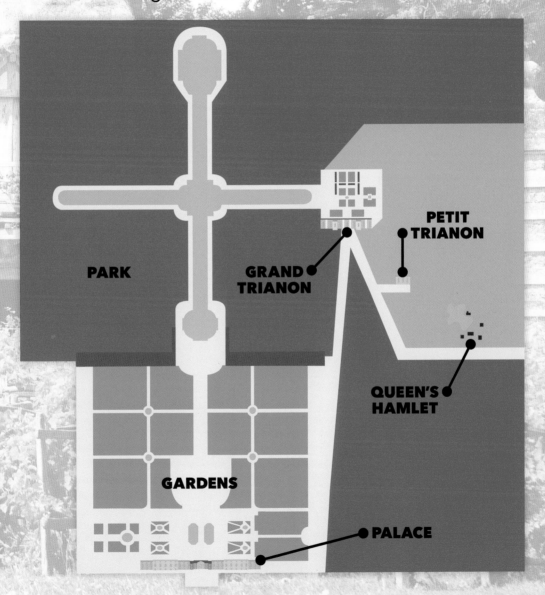

PARK

PETIT TRIANON

GRAND TRIANON

QUEEN'S HAMLET

GARDENS

PALACE

In October 1789, the king and queen hosted a fancy meal. Only **aristocrats** were invited. It angered the people of France. Many were poor and hungry. They marched to the palace to demand affordable food. Within days, the king and queen fled to Paris, France. It was a turning point of the French Revolution (1787–1799).

Now the palace is a museum. **Tourists** can see how the royalty of France once lived. Would you like to visit?

QUICK FACTS & TOOLS

PALACE OF VERSAILLES

Location: northern France

Years of Construction: 1661–1715

Size: 15.6 acres (6.3 hectares)

Number of Rooms: 2,300

Current Use: Open for tours

Average Number of Visitors Each Year: nearly 10 million

GLOSSARY

aristocrats: Members of a group of people thought to be the best in some way, usually based on their social class.

artisans: People who are skilled at working with their hands at a particular craft.

emblem: A symbol or a sign that represents something.

estate: A large area of land, usually with a house on it.

hamlet: A very small village.

lavish: Extravagant or luxurious.

reign: The ruling of a country as king or queen.

royal: Related to a king or queen or a member of his or her family.

throne: A special chair for a ruler to sit on during a ceremony.

topiaries: Plants that are cut or grown into decorative shapes.

tourists: People who travel and visit places for pleasure.

treaty: A formal written agreement between two or more countries.

INDEX

TO LEARN MORE

Finding more information is as easy as 1, 2, 3.

① Go to www.factsurfer.com

② Enter "PalaceofVersailles" into the search box.

③ Choose your book to see a list of websites.

FACT SURFER